The Weird, Wild and Wonderful Days of School

By

D. M. Larson

Copyright (c) 2013
All Rights Reserved

Contact doug@freedrama.net for questions about the script or permission to perform the play.

The Weird Wild and Wonderful Days of School

by D. M. Larson

CAST OF CHARACTERS

This play has a flexible cast. Not all scenes need to be performed. And actors can play multiple parts because no characters repeat from scene to scene. The smallest cast you could have by doing all the scripts would be three males and four females. But there are many as 49 speaking roles possible.

PRINCIPAL: A showy circus type announcer who introduces each scene.

SCENE 1: ROCK! SWORD! FIRECRACKER! (page 5)

MASTER: Master of the game of Rock, Sword, Firecracker

MEL and KELLY: Rock, Scissors, Paper Players.

OPTIONAL STUDENTS: If you have more actors, you can divide up Mel and Kelly's lines.

OPTIONAL ACTORS: Act out Rock, Sword, Firecracker scene

SCENE 2: KISS ME, I'M IRISH (page 9)

IRISH: a silly girl dressed up for St. Patrick's Day

SCOTTISH: a more serious girl who is grumpy

GUY: a flirtatious guy

ITALIAN: a hot headed girl who gets mad at guy

SCENE 3: BIG NOSE (page 12)

CAPTAIN: A bad actor who is a bully

SOLDIER: Another bad actor

CYRIL: A big nosed guy who uses words rather than fists to fight bullies

FRIEND: Cyril's friend in the audience

ROXY: A female actress who teases Cyril.

KELLY: The drama teacher who has no control.

SCENE 4: POLLY WANTS A CRACKER (page 22)

(CONTINUED)

CONTINUED: 2.

ANIMAL: A girl in an animal costume who likes the bird

BIRD: A guy in a bird costume who likes the animal back

SCENE 5: FARTZEN (page 29)

STEPH: Stressed out student (can be a man STEVE).

MASTER: Fart-Zen master who teaches relaxation techniques.

PUPIL: There can be one PUPIL or a dozen. Very flexible.

SCENE 6: THE BOY WHO CRIED GENIE (page 31)

DIRK: A male computer lab worker

GENIE: A magical creature who grants bad wishes

GIRL: A young looking playful girl

ZOMBIE: An old woman who is undead

WOMAN: She is good looking but turns out to be a vampire

JESI: A female computer lab worker

SCENE 7: ONE WAY OR ANOTHER (page 36)

JANE: A girl who used to date Ron

RON: A guy who wants to date Jane again.

SCENE 8: PITY THE FOOL (page 42)

JEORGE: The tricky artist with a secret plan.

SAGE: Cranky female friend of Mary

MARY: A girl who likes Jeorge's art

FRANK: A friend of Jeorge

SCENE 9: GIVING YOU MY HEART (page 47)

DAISY: A "special" girl who wants to make friends.

CARL: A "special" guy who likes everything in order.

ELMER: A "special" guy who is an artist.

SCENE 10: GOSSIP (page 49)

BULA: A student who thinks she is an ace reporter working at a major newspaper.

(CONTINUED)

CONTINUED: 3.

SKEETER: Assistant to Bula at the paper who forgets to do his job.

FANNY: a goofy female reporter who hangs out behind the boys locker room

MONITOR: sells his hall monitor reports

KILABREW: student assistant in nurse's office who loves to share medical related gossip

SCENE 11: LOOKS GET IN THE WAY (page 57)

SIDNEY: A woman who wants to find the perfect guy but wears a mask to hide how she looks.

TONY: A guy is scared off by Sidney.

WAITER/WAITRESS: No lines. Serves the food.

PHIL: A guy is isn't bothered by Sidney's mask.

OPTIONAL SCENE 12: MUCH MADNESS (page 67)

JANEY: A troubled student

REID: The doctor who tries to help her

NURSE: Assists Dr. Reid

OPTIONAL SCENE 13: FLOWERS IN THE DESERT (page 78)

JIMMY: A drunk kid in love with SHELLY

SHELLY: A troubled girl who isn't sure she likes JIMMY any more

JAMIE: Shelly's friend

SARGE: One of the caretakers of troubled kids at a group home in the desert. Former army sergeant.

****

PROLOGUE

The Principal comes out on stage looking more like an announcer at a circus than the principal of a school.

                     PRINCIPAL
         We welcome all kinds to our
         school... the weird, the wild...
                  (MORE)

(CONTINUED)

CONTINUED: 4.

> **PRINCIPAL (cont'd)**
> and the wonderful! We turn no one away. So many kids don't fit in these days, but in this school, one size fits all. No one is outcast, no one is forgotten... and if there isn't a class you want, we'll make one you do want.

Some kids gather.

> **PRINCIPAL (CONT.)**
> Here we are outside of school before the day starts. We see some of our students hanging out playing a well known game... but do they know as much about it as they think?

SCENE 1: ROCK! SWORD! FIRECRACKER!

Group of friends playing rock scissors paper. They all say:

> **ALL**
> Rock, scissors, paper!

They all do one of the above. One person gets rock and the rest get scissors and he/she pounds all their scissors. They all laugh and start another round. One person gets scissors and the rest paper and he/she cuts all their papers dramatically. There is Asian music and a person enters dressed in traditional Asian clothing. The players don't notice at first but the master shouts:

> **MASTER**
> Stop!

They all freeze.

> **KELLY**
> Who are you?

> **MASTER**
> I am the master of the Rock!

Master holds out a fist. Players all look at each other and then laugh.

> **MEL**
> Well, I've got paper.

(CONTINUED)

CONTINUED: 5.

Mel puts a flat hand over the Master's fist. Players laugh and then Master grabs Mel's hand and throws Mel on a table and sticks a finger to Mel's throat.

                    MASTER
     And I have sword.

                    KELLY
     There's no sword in Rock, Paper, Scissors.

                    MASTER
     That is where you are mistaken.

Master helps Mel up.

                    MASTER (CONT.)
     I am here to tell you the story of... (dramatic pause) ROCK! (holds up a fist) SWORD! (holds up index finger) FIRECRACKER! (holds up thumb).

Players all look at each other confused.

                    MEL
     I thought it was rock, scissors, paper.

                    MASTER
     You are wrong! The ancient game has been dishonored by scissors and paper. It is a mockery of the true art of the challenge. Shall I tell you the story?

                    KELLY
     Sure.

                    MASTER
     If you wish to hear the story, you must say, "Yes, Master."

They all look at each other, some shrug, some make funny face but they all nod in agreement.

                    ALL
     Yes, master.

                    MASTER
     Say... "Pretty please."

They give each other looks and then say.

(CONTINUED)

CONTINUED:

>   ALL
>   Pretty please.
>
>   MASTER
>   "Pretty please with a cherry
>   blossom on top."
>
>   MEL
>   Come on!
>
>   MASTER
>   Fine. I tell you the story.

The master can pull out a scroll or book to help with the story. This next part is flexible for staging. The master can act out his story, more actors can come in and act out the story or the players can act out the story.

>   MASTER (CONT.)
>   It all began with the rock.
>
>   KELLY
>   You mean like the wrestler?
>
>   MASTER
>   No, the rock was a big fat lazy
>   slob. But he was unmovable. He was
>   a champion sumo wrestler because no
>   one could move him. He won every
>   match. And then he sent a challenge
>   out to all warriors that no one
>   could defeat him. So samurai and
>   ninja from all over Asia came to
>   fight him, but even a sword could
>   piece his rock-like skin. But then
>   a magician from a distant land came
>   with a mighty weapon. A
>   firecracker! No one had seen such a
>   huge firecracker before. The
>   magician faced off against the
>   Rock. He lit fuse and placed it at
>   the Rock's feet. The Rock did not
>   care. He did not think anything
>   could defeat him. Suddenly, there
>   was a huge explosion. They were
>   screams and cries of pain. And when
>   the smoke cleared, the Rock had
>   fallen. Everyone stood quietly and
>   couldn't believe their eyes. A few
>   began to cry. The magician's laugh
>   broke the silence and he pulled
>   another, even bigger firecracker
>   from his ropes. The magician
>   (MORE)

(CONTINUED)

CONTINUED:

>   MASTER (cont'd)
>   yelled, "I shall rid this land of
>   the Rock forever!" He placed the
>   firecracker next to the Rock and
>   lit it. But then a young one, who
>   was a big fan and collected all the
>   Rock memorabilia, sprang in to
>   action. He snatched up a sword and
>   "swish", cut the fuse, saving the
>   rock from destruction.

The master bows to end his story and the players clap and cheer.

>   MEL
>   Amazing.
>
>   KELLY
>   Great story!
>
>   MASTER
>   So I ask that you no longer
>   dishonor the game with scissors and
>   paper.
>
>   MEL
>   Yes, Master!
>
>   KELLY
>   We will, Master. Master bows and
>   then leaves.
>
>   MEL
>   Ready?
>
>   ALL
>   Rock, sword, firecracker!

All except one do firecracker and one does sword and dramatically cuts their fuses with karate sounds.

>   KELLY
>   That is more fun.
>
>   ALL
>   Rock, sword, firecracker!

All except one do rock and one does dynamite and blows them up and they fall to the ground laughing.

>   END OF SCENE

Bell rings... students rush to class. Principal steps out.

(CONTINUED)

CONTINUED: 8.

> PRINCIPAL
> Now we move to the classrooms. We see a few students filter in to what we'd call a more typical classroom... well, more like a stereotypical classroom.

SCENE 2: KISS ME, I'M IRISH

There is an empty classroom with a table center with three chairs. A board or bulletin board says Happy St. Patrick's Day. Irish girl walks in and sits at the first chair. She has a "Kiss Me I'm Irish" shirt on and maybe a cute little green hat. She settles in with her book, notebook and pencil and looks around for cute guys when she is ready for class. Scottish girl walks in and has a sour look on her face. She sees Irish girl and gets an annoyed look. She sits two chairs down from her. She has on a shirt that says "Don't Kiss Me, I'm Scottish." After a few moments:

> SCOTTISH
> I hate St. Patrick's Day.

Irish girl looks at Scottish girl surprised.

> IRISH
> How come?

> SCOTTISH
> All the stupid shirts, wearing green, the green drinks... so disgusting. It makes a mockery of the true meaning of the holiday.

Irish girl gets a very confused look on her face.

> IRISH
> What is the true meaning of St. Patrick's Day?

> SCOTTISH
> See!

Irish girl looks around even more confused. Cute guy walks in and sits between them. Irish girl is all happy and gives him a big smile and tries to make sure he can see her shirt. Scottish girl crosses her arms.

> GUY
> Hey ladies. How you are you this fine St. Patrick's Day?

Irish girl giggles and Scottish girl rolls her eyes.

(CONTINUED)

CONTINUED: 9.

                    IRISH
          I'm Irish.

She giggles more and he leans in.

                    GUY
          Does that mean I should kiss you?

She giggles even more. Guy turns to Scottish girl.

                    GUY (CONT.)
          What's your shirt say?

Scottish girl puts down her arms.

                    GUY (CONT.)
          "Don't kiss me I'm Scottish."
          That's funny.

Guy takes off his glasses, turns up the smolder. Scottish girl gets nervous.

                    GUY (CONT.)
          So you don't want me to kiss you
          huh?

Scottish is nervous and unconvincing.

                    SCOTTISH
          No.

                    GUY
          No? You sure?

                    SCOTTISH
          No.

                    GUY
          Because I think your eyes are
          saying yes.

He leans in more, but then Italian rushes in.

                    ITALIAN
          What are you doing?

Guy sits up.

                    GUY
          What? Huh? Nothing.

(CONTINUED)

CONTINUED: 10.

                  ITALIAN
    I saw the way you were looking at
    her.

                  GUY
    No, I just needed a pencil.

Guy takes pencil from Scottish girl and shows it to Italian but she rips it out of her hand and throws it.

                  ITALIAN
    Get over here...

She points off left.

                  ITALIAN (CONT.)
    Now!

Guy jumps up and rushes off with her following. Irish and Scottish watch off left.

                  GUY (OFF)
    I'm sorry, I'm sorry!

Irish and Scottish look at each other.

                  IRISH AND SCOTTISH
    Italian.

                  IRISH
    She's definitely Italian.

                  END OF SCENE

Students leave and Principal enters.

                  PRINCIPAL
    Some teens try hard to fit in to a
    group while others embrace who they
    are. Still others fight the
    stereotypes they fall in to. Let's
    visit our drama classroom where a
    big nosed boy fights back against
    some kids who have tormented
    him. But he doesn't fight with
    fists... he fights with words.

SCENE 3: BIG NOSE

Drama kids bring out simple set. There is a balcony with odd colored cloth hanging down and a backdrop that is supposed to be a castle. Two students enter in Shakespearean type dress. They are very bad actors who think they are very good.

                    CAPTAIN
Look at yonder window, friend. She awaits me, she does.

                    SOLDIER
Doth she?

                    CAPTAIN
She does.

                    SOLDIER
But doth she love thee?

                    CAPTAIN
She does.

                    SOLDIER
So good for you.

                    CYRIL
        (From audience)
So bad for us!

He and FRIENDS laugh. The two actors take a quick glance out in surprise then quickly get back in character

                    CAPTAIN
Uh... yes. She loveth me. She wroteth a letter.
        (Takes it out. Sniffs lovingly)
Ah, doth though smelleth her fragrance? Doth thou find it heavenly?

                    SOLDIER
        (Excited)
I smell. I smell.

                    CYRIL
You can say that again.

He and friends laugh. The two actors try to hide their anger, but they don't do it well.

                                  (CONTINUED)

CONTINUED:

                    CAPTAIN
          Tonight, I shall go to her.
          Tonight. Tonight!

                    CYRIL
          When?!

                    CAPTAIN
              (Angry. Trying to be more
               dramatic)
          Tonight!

                    CYRIL
              (Mocking)
          I can't hear you.

                    CAPTAIN
          Quiet!

CAPTAIN is about to jump off the stage but SOLDIER grabs him.

                    SOLDIER
          I can not let you go to her.

                    CAPTAIN
              (One more look at MAN then
               gets back to play)
          Why doth thou stopeth me?

                    SOLDIER
          Because she is to be mine.

                    CAPTAIN
          Then we must fight to our deaths.

                    CYRIL
          We can only hope.

                    SOLDIER
              (They pull swords)
          We fight for love!

They dual. MAN sings "Love Boat Theme" or some other silly romance song. He gets FRIENDS to join in. CAPTAIN is stabbed.

                    CAPTAIN
          Oh, my heart. My loving heart. My
          heart is stabbed. I can love no
          more.

(CONTINUED)

SOLDIER
Oh, my captain. I have slain thee. But how?

CYRIL
What do you mean "how"? What's that in your hand, a swizzle stick?

CAPTAIN
I die now. I die. I leave thee to love for I can love no more. My heart is worn. My blood will pour this night no more. I leave my sword, my rank, my love. You have it all now. You have everything I desire.
　　(Cough)
I die and leave thee. I die and leave thee these words.

CYRIL
Will you just die already?!

CAPTAIN
　　(Jumps up)
I've had it with you!

CYRIL
It's a miracle. He's alive.

CAPTAIN
　　(Picks up his sword)
I've had it with you.

CYRIL jumps up on stage. He has a huge nose.

CYRIL
Remember me?

CAPTAIN
Oh, yeah. I know you now. You're the one with the big nose.

Gasp from CYRIL'S FRIENDS

FRIEND
　　(From audience)
You shouldn't have said that.

CYRIL
You're offended by my nose?

                    CAPTAIN
          It is no stranger than a dog with
          two tails.

He laughs but no one laughs with him

                    CYRIL
          There was a poem a read once. It
          goes something like this:
                    (Picking up a sword)
          "Roses are red. Violets are
          fuchsia. What you dish out, comes
          right back to ya!

(And CYRIL quickly unarms the CAPTAIN with a twist of his
sword

                    CAPTAIN
                    (Looks at empty hand)
          How did you...? (Backs away) No
          hard feeling, huh?

                    CYRIL
          None at all.

CAPTAIN starts to go

                    CYRIL
          See you in class tomorrow.

                    CAPTAIN
          Oh, no.

                    CYRIL
          Oh, yes. I transferred to this
          class.

                    CAPTAIN
          Oh, golly.

Captain exits.

                    ROXY
                    (Comes out on balcony)
          What's going on out here?

                    CYRIL
                    (To audience)
          Now, for the moment you've all been
          waiting for. The farewell. When we
          last left our hero, he was flat on
          the floor, bleeding and giving some
          terribly boring speech. But his
                         (MORE)

CONTINUED: 15.

>   CYRIL (cont'd)
>   fair lady comes out and sees him
>   dying. She calls out to him:

He points to her. Roxy gives him a dirty look.

>   ROXY
>   What is this?

>   CYRIL
>   And she says...

>   ROXY
>   (Sighs. Speaks flatly)
>   Oh, but I must have one good-bye
>   kiss.

>   CYRIL
>   And so our hero, though he is
>   bleeding to death, uses his last
>   bit of strength to climb up to her.
>   (He does actions. The ROXY
>   looks very annoyed. He is
>   almost to her)
>   He wants that one last kiss. The
>   kiss he has been dreaming of. But
>   before he can reach her he tosses
>   the mortal coil. UHHH! (He dies and
>   falls. Looks out at audience) And
>   dies. (Stands up) Finally.

>   ROXY
>   That isn't how it ends.

>   CYRIL
>   It isn't?

>   ROXY
>   No.
>   (She looks at him)
>   It ends with a kiss.

>   CYRIL
>   It does?

>   ROXY
>   Yes.

>   CYRIL
>   Really?
>   (He climbs up again)
>   Could you perhaps... show me?

(CONTINUED)

CONTINUED: 16.

She looks at him critically and then smiles. She leans to almost kiss him.

                         ROXY
               In your dreams.

She pushes him off. MS. KELLY rushes out and faces audience

                         KELLY
               Well, class... that uh... wasn't
               quite how the scene normally goes.

Captain stomps on stage all upset.

                         CAPTAIN
               I quit!

Captain stomps off.

                         KELLY
               Well, I guess we'll be recasting.
               Um... well, while we wait... uh...
               we'll...

                         CYRIL
               I'd be happy to recite some of my
               poetry for the class.

Captain comes back on.

                         CAPTAIN
               Poetry? Snore!

                         CYRIL
               You're still here? Did the rest of
               the theatre group leave town
               without you?

                         CAPTAIN
               Aren't you being a little nosey?
                    (Referring to CYRIL'S nose)
               I guess you're probably always
               nosing around. (CYRIL is mad. ROXY,
               SOLDIER, KELLY reappear on stage)
               What's wrong? I guess nobody nose!

                         CYRIL
               Is that all you can think up?

                         CAPTAIN
               I'm sure I could come up with a few
               more.

                                                         (CONTINUED)

CONTINUED:

CYRIL
I bet you can't.

CAPTAIN
Wanna bet?

CYRIL
Gladly. I challenge you to a dual of jokes. Whoever tells the most nose jokes...

CAPTAIN
Yes?

CYRIL
(Thinks. CYRIL motions to ROXY)
Gets a kiss from the lovely lady.

KELLY
Um... well... no!

ROXY
No, it's okay.

KELLY
Well, I guess if you are okay with it. Carry on class!

CAPTAIN
(Comes onstage. Eyeing ROXY)
I'll gladly accept as long as it's a real kiss, not one of those stage kisses.

ROXY
It depends how funny your jokes are.

CYRIL
Shall we begin?

CAPTAIN
Okay, big nose.
(Laughs)
There's one.

CYRIL
That's it? I guess I shouldn't expect much from someone who must use his nose to count to eleven.

(CONTINUED)

CONTINUED: 18.

>   FRIEND
>   (From audience)
>   One - one!
>
>   CYRIL
>   No, no. We are insulting my nose,
>   not his. Let's see. Oh, yes.
>   Aggressive: Sir, if I had such a
>   nose, I would cut it off to please,
>   not spite, my face.
>   (Looks at audience)
>   One - one.
>
>   CAPTAIN
>   Your nose is so big you must use a
>   box of tissues a day.
>   (A few boos from FRIENDS)
>
>   CYRIL
>   Oh, let's give it to him. Two -
>   one.
>   (Thinks)
>   Hmmm. Ah, here's one: Hey, that
>   thing's nearly a house... and wow,
>   what a view!
>
>   FRIEND
>   Two - two!
>
>   CAPTAIN
>   (Frustrated. Then smiles)
>   I've seen a bigger nose. On an
>   elephant.
>
>   CYRIL
>   Very good. Three - two.
>   (Thinks. Smiles)
>   On exercise: I've heard of people
>   developing their muscles, but
>   developing your nose? It's the
>   noseflex exercise challenge.
>
>   FRIEND
>   Three all!
>
>   CAPTAIN
>   (Annoyed)
>   Uh, your nose is so big you...
>   you...
>
>   CYRIL
>   See the snot before you hear the
>   sneeze?

(CONTINUED)

CONTINUED:

>   FRIEND
> That point goes to Cyril.
>
>   CAPTAIN
> He didn't let me finish.
>
>   CYRIL
> Go ahead.
>
>   CAPTAIN
> It's so big... you're always nosing around.
>   (Boos)
>
>   CYRIL
> No point.
>   (CAPTAIN scowls)
> Gracious: How kind of you! How many people put a bird perch on his face?
>
>   CAPTAIN
> Now look here...
>
>   CYRIL
> When you have a cigarette and blow out your nose, do the neighbors cry, "Look out! A chimney's on fire!"
>
>   CAPTAIN
> Forget it... I'm through...
>
>   CYRIL
>   (Stops him)
> But I'm just getting started. When you go to the movies, do they charge you twice?
>
>   FRIEND
> Seven to three!
>
>   CAPTAIN
> It is not!
>
>   CYRIL
>   (CAPTAIN is really ticked)
> And for my final insult: Musical. Sing with me now: (FRIENDS sing) Nobody NOSE the trouble I've seen. Nobody NOSE my sorrow.

FRIENDS give wild applause

(CONTINUED)

CONTINUED:

>   CAPTAIN
>   I'm out of here.
>
>   CYRIL
>   Don't forget to write.
>
>   ROXY
>   Its about time somebody put that
>   jerk in his place.
>   (Smiles at CYRIL who suddenly
>   becomes shy)
>   And for your prize...
>
>   CYRIL
>   A kiss?
>
>   ROXY
>   Yup. Close your eyes.

Cyril gets excited and closes his eyes. Roxy gives him a
big smile and then she gives him a chocolate candy kiss.

>   CYRIL
>   Funny.
>
>   ROXY
>   I thought so.
>
>   END OF SCENE

Drama students clear the set. Principal enters.

>   PRINCIPAL
>   A candy kiss is sweeter than no
>   kiss at all. I think Shakepeare
>   said something like that. Now what
>   school would be complete without
>   school fund raisers. School fund
>   raisers pay for much of what you
>   see here at our school... and even
>   paid for my new car! Kidding on
>   that last part. But school fund
>   raising also provides another
>   social outlet for our students who
>   are just looking to connect with
>   someone... giving one odd bird a
>   chance to meet another.

SCENE 4: POLLY WANTS A CRACKER

Two teens are in a mall selling products. The guy named Carl is in a fat bird costume selling some kind of candy. The girl named Polly is in an animal costume selling animal crackers. The bird man keeps checking out the animal woman but not so bad that she doesn't seem to notice... but eventually she does. She goes up to him.

>ANIMAL
>I have to say... that costume is really cute.

>BIRD
>What? Uh... really?

>ANIMAL
>I love chunky birds... I just want to squeeze them.

She gets embarrassed and goes back to her animal cracker sale table. He mumbles under his breath.

>BIRD
>You can squeeze me if you want.

She hears.

>ANIMAL
>What? He is startled and turns away.

>BIRD
>Nothing.

She looks kind of sad and turns away. He decides to talk to her some more.

>BIRD
>So what are you selling?

She is happy he is talking to her again.

>ANIMAL
>Animal crackers.

>BIRD
>Oh, I love animal crackers.

>ANIMAL
>Want to buy some?

He tries to get to his wallet but can't because of the bird costume.

(CONTINUED)

CONTINUED:

                    BIRD
          Yeah... oh crap, I don't think I
          can reach my wallet.

                    ANIMAL
          I can help.

                    BIRD
          If you reach in the opening in the
          back...

She reach in back and someone walks by and stops... stares.
She gets mad at the person who is staring at them.

                    ANIMAL
          What?!

Person runs off.

                    BIRD
          Got my wallet?

                    ANIMAL
          Yup... so you're not fat? He
          laughs.

                    BIRD
          No... disappointed?

                    ANIMAL
          No... I like fat birds, not fat
          guys.

                    BIRD
          Good... because I'm not fat... not
          that you want to like me... I'm not
          saying that you have to like me...
          I mean...

She closes his bird mouth over his face.

                    ANIMAL
          You're cute.

She lets go. He is confused.

                    BIRD
          Huh?

                    ANIMAL
          Nothing. So you want one box or
          two... of animal crackers?

                                                  (CONTINUED)

CONTINUED: 23.

>   BIRD
>   How much money do I have in my
>   wallet?
>
>   ANIMAL
>   A lot... you rich or something?
>
>   BIRD
>   You like rich guys?
>
>   ANIMAL
>   Not really.
>
>   BIRD
>   Then all that money is stolen.
>
>   ANIMAL
>   I don't like thieves either.
>
>   BIRD
>   Stolen but I recovered it from the
>   thieves and I'm returning it to the
>   rightful owner.
>
>   ANIMAL
>   There you go! I knew you were a
>   good simple honest... bird.
>
>   BIRD
>   Those crackers look good... wish I
>   could eat some now. These bird
>   hands are a pain. I try to eat and
>   the wing smacks me in the face.

He demonstrates and she laughs.

>   ANIMAL
>   I can feed them to you.

He gets all embarrassed at her offer.

>   BIRD
>   Really? You mean with your hands...
>   in my mouth.
>
>   ANIMAL
>   Sure, why not?
>
>   BIRD
>   Wow... well, uh... okay.

She feeds him. He gets a very funny look on his face.

(CONTINUED)

CONTINUED:

>   ANIMAL
>   You okay?

>   BIRD
>   Uh... that was so nice... I mean
>   good... yummy... I mean...

>   ANIMAL
>   What is with you?

>   BIRD
>   You're really nice.

>   ANIMAL
>   Oh... thank you. Here let me put
>   your wallet back...

She puts it back and checks out his rear.

>   BIRD
>   So...

>   ANIMAL
>   Want another cracker?

>   BIRD
>   Sure!

She feeds him again and he flaps his wings happily.

>   ANIMAL
>   You like them?

>   BIRD
>   Yummy.

>   ANIMAL
>   I like to bite off their heads. Am
>   I sick?

>   BIRD
>   That's funny actually.

>   ANIMAL
>   How are sales going?

>   BIRD
>   Good... only one box left to sell.

>   ANIMAL
>   I have tons... I guess I'll be by
>   myself soon.

(CONTINUED)

CONTINUED:

She looks in sales box. Person comes back to buy the Bird's last box. He hides his box.

          BIRD
I'm out... beat it.

Person leaves annoyed.

          ANIMAL
That's what I was afraid of. Tons left. I'll be here forever. I think my costume is scaring people away. I wish I had a cute birdie costume like you. I wanna squeeze you so bad.

          BIRD
Go for it.

          ANIMAL
Really?

          BIRD
Squeeze away.

She rushes up and grabs him and gives him a huge hug. She squeals in delight.

          ANIMAL
That was... awesome!

Bird is in a happy daze.

          BIRD
Yeah.

          ANIMAL
Good birdie... here's a cracker... (he flaps his wings) ...you really like it when I feed you don't you?

          BIRD
Yeah.

          ANIMAL
So what you doing after school?

          BIRD
Wanna go eat something maybe... you wanna come feed me some more?

(CONTINUED)

ANIMAL
In your dreams...

BIRD
Yeah.

ANIMAL
Okay.

BIRD
What?

ANIMAL
I'll go out with you.

BIRD
Really?

ANIMAL
I think you're cute.

BIRD
But you don't even know exactly what I look like... I look like some guy who is getting barfed by a bird.

ANIMAL
I saw your driver's license picture...

BIRD
That's even worse. And you still like me? That picture is terrible.

ANIMAL
Well, if you look better than that picture, we're in business.

BIRD
You're funny.

ANIMAL
I know.

BIRD
So if you sell the rest of those crackers, you can go?

ANIMAL
Yes, but that might take forever.

CONTINUED:

     BIRD
I think I'd like to buy some more crackers.

     ANIMAL
How many more?

     BIRD
All of them.

     ANIMAL
You don't have to do that.

     BIRD
I'm rich remember?

     ANIMAL
I thought you stole that money.

     BIRD
No, I'm a superhero who recovered the stolen cash.

     ANIMAL
Oh, that's right. Birdman?

     BIRD
I'm unflappable.

     ANIMAL
Nice... you need your own comic book.

     BIRD
So how about it? Sell me those crackers?

     ANIMAL
You're serious?

     BIRD
I really want to take you out.

     ANIMAL
What we having? Crackers?

     BIRD
Cheese and crackers?

     ANIMAL
Crackers a la mode?

CONTINUED: 28.

>   BIRD
>   Barbecued crackers?
>
>   ANIMAL
>   Baked crackers?
>
>   BIRD
>   You crack me up.

They walk out together happily.

                        END OF SCENE

Principal enters.

>   PRINCIPAL
>   Fund raising love... that scene
>   made me crack a smile. Now to gym
>   class where they exercise more than
>   muscles. Some of our student get a
>   little too serious and need to
>   relax and relieve some tension.
>   Stephanie Miller is one of those
>   students and we have a class just
>   for her.

SCENE 5: FART-ZEN

Lights come up on gym class. PUPILS are dressed in white and are in various strange positions in a state of meditation. Each PUPIL has a small box next to them. NOTE: There can be one PUPIL or a dozen. The Fart-Zen MASTER stands before them also in a state of meditation. STEPH enters. STEPH is the kind of student who always studies and never has fun. Everything about her scream tension. She stops worried she has interrupted them.

>   STEPH
>   Oh, I'm so sorry. I didn't realize
>   you were in the middle of a class.
>   I'll come back.
>
>   MASTER
>   No, please enter. All are welcome
>   here.
>
>   STEPH
>   Hello, I'm Stephanie Miller. Here
>   is my honor society ID card.

Pulls out a business card and gives it to the MASTER. STEPH turns and looks at PUPILS. MASTER tosses card carelessly.

(CONTINUED)

CONTINUED: 29.

> STEPH (CONT.)
> I was referred here by the counselor. She says I've got way too much stress in my life and she prescribed some relaxation exercises. Your Fart-Zen class comes highly recommended for it's success in relieving all kinds of stress and anxiety disorders.

STEPH has been pacing nervously. MASTER stops her.

> MASTER
> It is said "far-zen".

> STEPH
> Oh... so sorry. T is silent. Got it. Kind of like Mozart but the opposite. He must have taken your T sound.

> MASTER
> Perhaps. Pupils. Assume position... Ichi.

PUPILS all shift into a similar position and all fart as they do so. NOTE: The farting will most likely will have to be done with a recording unless you have some really talented farters in the cast. STEPH looks at them in disgust but MASTER says nothing.

> MASTER
> So what is the source of your tension?

> STEPH
> Huh? Oh, homework I guess.

> MASTER
> You seem distracted.

> STEPH
> Every since I got the honors classes, I've been a total air head.

> MASTER
> Position Ni!

PUPILS shift again to a new position and fart more.

(CONTINUED)

CONTINUED: 30.

                    STEPH
          Are they okay?

                    MASTER
          They are reaching a state of
          advanced relaxation. (To PUPILS)
          Refuel!

PUPILS sit by their boxes and pull out various things to
consume such as bean burritos, soda, broccoli, apples, milk,
cheese, etc.

                    STEPH
          Wait a minute. What is exactly the
          whole idea here?

                    MASTER
          All tension is something that is
          within you. Stress becomes bottled
          up and new stress makes it all
          shaken and builds inside you. If
          you have to way to relieve that
          stress, then it grows until it
          becomes unhealthy and even painful.
          Is your tension causing you pain?

                    STEPH
          It does. I get these panic
          attacks... I swear I was having a
          heart attack.

                    MASTER
          And one day you may unless you have
          a proper way to expel the demon
          which festers within.(To PUPILS)
          Prepare for the next position!

PUPILS rush excitedly and get themselves set.

                    MASTER (CONT.)
          Position San!

PUPILS bend in various positions and there is a some serious
farting.

                    STEPH
          Oh, man!

The smell is too much for STEPH and she covers her mouth.

                    MASTER
          We must all reach a state of
          perfect relaxation. But only the
                    (MORE)

                                                        (CONTINUED)

CONTINUED:

>   MASTER (cont'd)
>   Fert-zen master can achieve such a
>   perfect state through repeated
>   practice. The goal of all Fert-zen
>   students is to reach position Shi.
>
>   PUPILS
>   Show us, Master. Show us position
>   Shi.
>
>   STEPH
>   No, that's okay... I...
>
>   MASTER
>   Prepare for position Shi.

PUPILS all clear floor and wait excitedly as MASTER gets in a strange position. Long pause. Suddenly the fart comes quietly then builds and gets stronger. The PUPILS are in ecstacy. STEPH leaves in disgust. The fart grows and lights fade to black. The fart builds and then stops. Then continues after a moment almost explosively. The PUPILS clap. Wait for silence from audience and then a little fart then comes again just to finish it off. Wait for silence again. Slight pause.

>   PUPIL
>   You are the master.

Principal enters with hand pinching nose.

>   PRINCIPAL
>   Smells like success to me. Next we
>   go to our computer lab. Currently
>   we can only afford one computer but
>   the students love it. Everyone is
>   wishing for a chance to use
>   it. But wishes are tricky things.
>   Be careful what you wish for.

SCENE 6: THE BOY WHO CRIED GENIE

DIRK, a cool, confident guy, enters the lab. JESI, a shy, nerdy gal, looks like she wants to talk to him but can only manage a whisper.

>   JESI
>   Hi.

CONTINUED: 32.

DIRK doesn't hear her and goes to a computer to start work. Jesi rushes out all embarrassed. DIRK finds a cd stuck in the computer. It comes out and it is glowing [Light shines on it]. He looks at it and rubs it. A puff of smoke [fog machine] flows in and a Genie steps in with it.

                      GENIE
            What do you want?

                      DIRK
            What? Who are you?

DIRK lowers the cd and sees the Genie.

                      GENIE
            I'm a genie.

She waves her hands and more smoke appears.

                      DIRK
            A genie? So... does that mean I get
            three wishes?

                      GENIE
            Yeah, yeah. You know the drill.

                      DIRK
            Cool. Oh, I know what I want. I
            want the perfect girl.

                      GENIE
            As you wish...

Genie disappears into the smoke [exits] and GIRL appears, acting very young, licking a lollipop, hold a stuffed animal and jumping up and down excited.

                      GIRL
            Hi, let's play.

Dirk turns looking for the Genie.

                      DIRK
            No, no, no.

Genie appears and makes GIRL disappear [exits].

                      GENIE
            You did ask for a girl.

                      DIRK
            I want someone much older than
            that.

                                                  (CONTINUED)

CONTINUED: 33.

> GENIE
> As you wish...

Genie disappears [exits] and ZOMBIE appears.

> DIRK
> Not that old!

Genie makes Zombie disappear [exits].

> GENIE
> You're down to one wish... make it good.

> DIRK
> What? Oh, man. Okay. I want the perfect woman that is my age, beautiful and sharp.

> GENIE
> You got it.

Genie disappears and a beautiful WOMAN appears. She comes up to him and he smiles. She crosses behind him. She pushes back her hair and we see her pointed ears and she bares her fangs.

> WOMAN
> Want to neck?

DIRK smiles big and turns and sees her fangs come at him. He screams.

> DIRK
> Genie!

WOMAN disappears and Genie appears and sighs.

> WOMAN
> She wasn't sharp enough for you?

> DIRK
> You ruined all my wishes!

> GENIE
> Wishes are not the key to your happiness. Sometimes you just have to open your eyes and see the good things around you that are already here.

Genie disappears and DIRK falls into a chair. Jesi returns. She nervously approaches DIRK and touches him on the shoulder and he jumps.

(CONTINUED)

CONTINUED:

>   JESI
>   I'm sorry. Have you seen my keys.
>
>   DIRK
>   Keys?
>
>   JESI
>   Here they are.
>
>   DIRK
>   Hey, what's your name?
>
>   JESI
>   Jesi. And you're Dirk.
>
>   DIRK
>   You use the computer lab in the
>   mornings huh?
>
>   JESI
>   Uh-huh. You want my email? In case
>   you need to ask me something...
>   about the lab.
>
>   DIRK
>   I don't mind sharing... if you want
>   to stay and hang out?
>
>   JESI
>   Sure, I'd like that.

DIRK tosses the cd of the genie in the trash.

>   JESI (CONT.)
>   What was that?
>
>   DIRK
>   Some computer virus.
>
>   JESI
>   I know this great anti-virus
>   software... let me show you. It
>   works like magic.

                    END OF SCENE

>   PRINCIPAL
>   Magic indeed. It's not really
>   magic we need but a new look on the
>   world. We need to open our eyes to
>   see what's really important and
>   what really matters. Sometimes
>   it's been right in front of us all
>   (MORE)

(CONTINUED)

CONTINUED: 35.

> **PRINCIPAL (cont'd)**
> along. And sometimes we find what we want and then lose it again. That's where healing is needed. What better place to experience healing than in our nurse's office. But you'll find there is more than cuts and bruises healing there. Sometimes help is needed to heal the heart.

SCENE 7: ONE WAY OR ANOTHER

Jane is hurt and in nurse's office. Ron comes in and peeks around curtain.

> **JANE**
> What are you doing out here?

> **RON**
> I wanted to say hi.

> **JANE**
> Hi... bye.

> **RON**
> You look good.

> **JANE**
> Yeah, so.

> **RON**
> Very good.

> **JANE**
> Stop it.

> **RON**
> What?

> **JANE**
> We broke up, remember?

> **RON**
> Yeah.

> **JANE**
> YOU broke up with me.

> **RON**
> Yeah... you look good.

(CONTINUED)

                    JANE
          What's wrong?

                    RON
          I miss you.

                    JANE
          Well... I could be mean about it...
          and take pleasure you in saying
          that... and torment you... but... I
          miss you too...

                    RON
          You do?

                    JANE
          Yeah...

                    RON
          Can I come in?

He peaks around curtain.

                    JANE
          No.

                    RON
          Please.

                    JANE
          Go away.

                    RON
          But you miss me.

                    JANE
          Not that much.

                    RON
          I guess I shouldn't have got you
          anything then.

                    JANE
          You got me something?

                    RON
          Never mind... I'll go.

                    JANE
          But...you got me something.

CONTINUED:

>   RON
>   It's not much.
>
>   JANE
>   What is it?
>
>   RON
>   You want to see?
>
>   JANE
>   Yes.
>
>   RON
>   Can I come in?
>
>   JANE
>   No.
>
>   RON
>   Please.
>
>   JANE
>   Hold it up and I'll grab it.
>
>   RON
>   Really?
>
>   JANE
>   Yeah.

Ron tries to reach over curtain but they can't so he starts to climb up on something. She manages to grab it and he falls.

>   RON
>   Ah!
>
>   JANE
>   You okay?
>
>   RON
>   ...maybe
>
>   JANE
>   You're hurt?
>
>   RON
>   ...no... not much.
>
>   JANE
>   You look hurt.

(CONTINUED)

CONTINUED:

                    RON
          No... I'm fine.

                    JANE
          Why you still in the floor then?

                    RON
          It's comfortable. Think I'll just
          stay here a bit... enjoy the gift.

                    JANE
          I'm coming.

                    RON
          No, no... I don't want to bug
          you... see you later... I'm sure
          I'll be gone... eventually. One way
          or another.

Jane appears out front door and goes to bushes. She struggles to get him up.

                    JANE
          You are hurt.

                    RON
          That's not blood... that's
          uh...ketchup... had some fries at
          lunch.

                    JANE
          I didn't think you fell that
          hard. What did you land on?

                    RON
          I'm accident prone.

                    JANE
          I know. You need a keeper.

                    RON
          Want to be my keeper again?

He snuggles up to her.

                    JANE
          No.

She drops him.

                    RON
          Ow.

(CONTINUED)

CONTINUED:

>   JANE
>   Sorry.

She helps him up.

>   RON
>   You don't have to be nice to me
>   anymore.

>   JANE
>   I'll always be nice to you.

>   RON
>   Really? But I broke up with you.

>   JANE
>   That's right. I guess I should be a
>   little meaner. Good-bye.

>   RON
>   You're leaving?

>   JANE
>   You're not hurt that badly.

>   RON
>   Right.

>   JANE
>   See ya.

She goes to the door and exits. Ron tries standing and is in pain. His leg is probably broken. He struggles to walk but fails gloriously and falls. He crawls under a table dramatically and covers himself up. Suddenly there is a gasp of happiness and Jane rushes back in.

>   JANE (CONT.)
>   Ron? Ron, you there?

>   RON (OFF)
>   Maybe.

>   JANE
>   Where did you find these?

Ron tries to get up and pose like he isn't hurt.

>   RON
>   Oh those? No big deal. Just found
>   them.

(CONTINUED)

                    JANE
          These are my favorite chocolates...
          they only sell these in Europe.

                    RON
          Oh, really?

                    JANE
          Shut up. You knew.

                    RON
          You always carry on about them.
          Always wanted to get them for you.

                    JANE
          Why now?

                    RON
          Why now...

Ron turns sadly and starts to walk away and falls
dramatically.

                    JANE
          Oh no.

Jane goes to him.

                    RON
          I'm sorry. I didn't want to do this
          to you.

                    JANE
          Then why are you?

                    RON
          Because I miss you. I thought I was
          doing the right thing, but I miss
          you.

                    JANE
          I miss you too... but it hurt.

                    RON
          I know.

                    JANE
          You said so many things that hurt.

                    RON
          I thought you'd be better off
          without me.

(CONTINUED)

CONTINUED: 41.

                    JANE
          And you thought you'd be better off
          without me.

                    RON
          But I'm not.

Jane holds him.

                    JANE
          What am I going to do with you?

                    RON
          What am I going to do without you?

                    JANE
          How about I just sit here and hold
          you for awhile?

                    RON
          I'd like that.

Jane holds Ron closer.

Principal enters...

                    PRINCIPAL
          Where is that nurse? Oh well. The
          healing happened without her I
          think. At least the hurt is bit
          less... hurty. Sometimes love is
          an art form. And only a true
          artist can force cupid's
          bow. Let's take a look at art
          class where on such artist is at
          work.

SCENE 8: PITY THE FOOL

A guy, JEORGE, hangs on the wall as a part of a modern art
piece. People walk through the class and look at the odd
pieces of modern art. A couple of students, SAGE and MARY
stop at the man.

                    SAGE
          What's this?

                    MARY
          It's called "Pity the Fool."

                                                  (CONTINUED)

CONTINUED: 42.

>   SAGE
>   It's amazing. It looks so lifelike.
>
>   MARY
>   It's like he could walk right out
>   of the painting and talk to us.

Suddenly Jeorge's eyes pop open and the women are startled.

>   JEORGE
>   Do you have any water?

His eyes close again. Sage and Mary look at each other and then the painting again.

>   SAGE
>   You heard that right?
>
>   MARY
>   Yeah.
>
>   JEORGE
>   Water.
>
>   SAGE
>   I'll get some water.

Sage leaves. Mary wants to follow and doesn't want to be left alone.

>   JEORGE
>   Wait. Please.

Mary reluctantly stops. She looks around but is alone. She cautiously returns.

>   MARY
>   What? Uh... who? I mean...
>
>   JEORGE
>   Why am I here?
>
>   MARY
>   Sure... let's ask that question.
>
>   JEORGE
>   This is my self portrait.
>
>   MARY
>   Pity the fool?

(CONTINUED)

CONTINUED: 43.

>   JEORGE
>   Yes.
>
>   MARY
>   Well... it's working. I feel sorry
>   for you.
>
>   JEORGE
>   Everyone does.
>
>   MARY
>   Oh...

Mary looks around nervously hoping Sage will return. Jeorge climbs down off the background and sits at the edge of the art looking very hurt and sad. Sage returns with some bottled water.

>   SAGE
>   Found some water.

Jeorge takes it from her and gives a weak smile.

>   JEORGE
>   Thank you.

Jeorge drinks and lets the water refresh him. Mary and Sage look at each other and then at Jeorge nervously.

>   MARY
>   So uh... this is a self-portrait.
>
>   SAGE
>   You're the artist?
>
>   JEORGE
>   Yes.
>
>   SAGE
>   I have to say I've never seen
>   anything like this.
>
>   JEORGE
>   It's a variation on the living
>   statue idea.
>
>   MARY
>   So not original?
>
>   JEORGE
>   Not really.

They are all quiet a moment.

(CONTINUED)

CONTINUED:
                                                        44.

                    SAGE
          Well, I've never seen anything like
          it.

                    JEORGE
          Then you haven't been out much.

                    SAGE
          What? Look, we're trying to be
          nice.

                    JEORGE
          Because you pity me.

                    MARY
          That's what you want isn't it?

                    JEORGE
          How do you know what I want?!

Sage and Mary start to back away. Jeorge curls up at the bottom of his art.

                    SAGE
          Look. I think you're a little too
          much of a method artist.

Jeorge is starting to cry.

                    MARY
          Is he crying?

                    SAGE
          Let's get out of here before he
          totally flips out.

                    MARY
          But he's so sad.

                    SAGE
          It's some twisted performance art I
          think.

                    MARY
          You have to admit. It's pretty
          original.

                    SAGE
          Just because it is different,
          doesn't mean it's good.

Jeorge looks up sadly at Sage.

                                                (CONTINUED)

CONTINUED:

>   JEORGE
>   You... you don't think it's good?
>
>   SAGE
>   Let's go.

Sage tries to go but Mary doesn't leave.

>   MARY
>   I think it's one of the most
>   interesting things I've ever seen.
>
>   JEORGE
>   You're just saying that to be nice.
>   You don't really feel that way.
>
>   MARY
>   I do. Really. Art is always so
>   bland and two dimensional. Your
>   work is so... alive... literally.

Jeorge gives Sage a pouty look.

>   JEORGE
>   She hates it though. Sage gives him
>   a dirty look and Jeorge gets sad
>   and collapses in to his art.
>
>   MARY
>   Say something nice to him.
>
>   SAGE
>   What? No.
>
>   MARY
>   Do it.

Sage reluctantly goes up to Jeorge. Mary pushes her closer and Sage slaps her hand away. Sage is next to him.

>   SAGE
>   Okay, I have to admit. This is the
>   most unusual... (Mary pokes her)
>   ...different... most creative piece
>   of art here tonight.

Jeorge says weakly:

>   JEORGE
>   Thank you.

Sage turns to Mary and pulls her away.

CONTINUED:

>   SAGE
>   Can we go now?
>
>   MARY
>   You go. I'll catch up in a minute.
>
>   SAGE
>   Whatever.

Sage leaves. Mary goes up to Jeorge and kneels down next to him.

>   MARY
>   What happened to you that inspired
>   this?

Jeorge sits up slowly and looks up at his background.

>   JEORGE
>   It's a long story. Everything you
>   see here represents something
>   that's happen in my life that has
>   brought me to this point.
>
>   MARY
>   The images are stunning. I've never
>   seen a work of art with so much
>   story to it. I could probably sit
>   here for hours trying to figure it
>   all out.
>
>   JEORGE
>   Stay then.
>
>   MARY
>   I have to go... how long will you
>   be... on display?
>
>   JEORGE
>   This is the last day. I have to
>   take it home today.

Mary writes her number on a piece of paper and gives it to him..

>   MARY
>   I would like to see you... and your
>   work again. Here's my number. Call
>   me... so I can see it again.
>
>   JEORGE
>   I will.

(CONTINUED)

CONTINUED: 47.

> MARY
> I better go. Great work on this.
> It's very moving.

Jeorge gives a weak smile and waves good-bye as Mary leaves. He climbs back up in to his original position. Frank enters and goes up to Jeorge.

> FRANK
> You got another number didn't you?

> JEORGE
> Yup.

> FRANK
> There has to be an easier way to get a date.

> JEORGE
> What can I say. I'm a fool.

> FRANK
> Ain't that the truth.

END OF SCENE

Principal enters.

> PRINCIPAL
> That was the art of something. But is that really the best way to fall in love? Sometimes it takes something very special to make that happen and where better to find that special place than in a very special classroom in our school. We call it special education because something very special happens there every day.

SCENE 9: GIVING YOU MY HEART

There is a classroom with a bunch of chairs. Carl enters and starts arranging them in a circle. They have to be perfectly in line and spaced or he isn't happy. Elmer enters and grabs a chair out of the circle and moves it totally out of alignment. Carl gets upset and starts pacing. He goes toward Elmer but then stops and goes back to chairs. But he can't focus on anything but Elmer's chair so he goes back and forth. Meanwhile Elmer gets out a notebook, pencil and eraser. He sharpens the pencil and let's the shavings fall on the floor. Carl runs to get a trash can and puts it under

(CONTINUED)

CONTINUED:

the sharpener. Elmer inspects the pencil. Carl steps away. Elmer sharpens more on other side. Carl rushes to move can but Elmer stops and starts drawing. Daisy enters. She is chewing on her fingers and her hair is a mess. She rushes to the nearest chair and grabs the seat to make herself stop chewing. Carl gets to her and looks at her nervously. She sees his chair pattern and moves her chair to fit his circle. Carl finishes and then paces back and forth between Elmer and Daisy. He walks away from the chair, makes upset sounds and sticks his fingers in his ears. He calms and then returns. Elmer doesn't move. He walks away again, plugs his ears and hums. Finally he returns. He starts pulling at his nose and moaning louder. Daisy sits and rocks nervously. Daisy looks back and forth to Carl and Elmer. She gets up and immediately chews on her fingers. Daisy goes and moves her chair next to Elmer so it aligns to a new pattern. She then moves another chair and tries to grab Carl. He won't let her grab him but follows her to the chair. Daisy fixes the other chairs to align to a new pattern to meet both Elmer and Carl's expectations. Carl walks once around the circle and adjust a few chairs and then sits happily. Daisy sits between Carl and Elmer. They all sit quietly a moment. Daisy gets some hearts out of her purse. They are big homemade heart cards. She holds one out to Elmer. He ignores her. She holds one out to Carl.

                    DAISY
     I'm giving you my heart.

He looks at it suspiciously. He suddenly grabs it cobra fast, so fast that Daisy is startled. Carl looks at the heart and folds it in half. He rushes to find some scissors in the room. He finds some and starts trimming the heart to make it a perfect heart shape. Daisy watches sadly. Elmer is getting a new pencil sharpened. Daisy goes up to him and looks at his picture.

                    DAISY
     A Princess.

Elmer is startled. He throws down his pencil and covers the picture.

                    ELMER
     I hate it.

                    DAISY
     It's... pretty.

                    ELMER
     I hate it.

(CONTINUED)

CONTINUED:

Elmer stuffs it in the garbage can. Then he quickly gathers his stuff and jams it into his bag. Daisy steps back and bites her fingers and rocks. Elmer is making angry sounds and starts pushing chairs around. Carl stands up and drops the tiny heart he has left after cutting it repeatedly and gasps. Daisy goes to the garbage can. She debates about getting it out but can't bring herself to pull it out. She bends down and looks at it.

                    DAISY
          Pretty.

Carl grabs two or three chairs and makes a little fort for himself to hide in upstage. Elmer falls to the floor with his bag clutched to him. He's shaking. Daisy gets another heart out of her purse. She cautiously goes to Elmer and sits near him. She holds out the heart to him. Elmer starts crying.

                    DAISY
          I'm giving you my heart.

Elmer turns to her and instead of taking the heart he embraces her and holds her tight, almost to the point of where she feels she might break. She struggles but doesn't want him to let go. She struggles to bring her arms down to hold him back. Finally after much effort, she does.

                 END OF SCENE

Principal enters.

                    PRINCIPAL
          Now we go from a place where they
          say very little to a place where
          they say too much... on to the
          school newspaper.... where gossip
          is news and facts are merely a
          rumor.

SCENE 10: GOSSIP

Play takes place in a makeshift newspaper office. BULA sits at her desk facing the audience and SKEETER is sleeping under a table covered by newspapers.

                    BULA
          Skeeeeeter! Where are you?

Skeeter Crawls out from under a table

                    SKEETER
          Yeah.

                    BULA
          What you doin' down there?

                    SKEETER
          Sleepin'.

                    BULA
          Didn't you go home last night?

                    SKEETER
          We had a deadline for the school
          paper. Pulled an all nighter.

                    BULA
          So you got the paper done? Where is
          it?

                    SKEETER
          [Looks] Shoot. I knew I forgot
          something.

                    BULA
          Now, Skeeter....

                    SKEETER
          Oowa, baby. The "Now Skeeter" talk.

                    BULA
          We have an obligation to the
          students of this school to bring
          them news on a weekly basis.
          [SKEETER mouths the speech as he
          sits and listens] We are this
          school's ear to the world. They
          count on us to give them the news
          like no one else can... You
          listenin' to me, Skeeter? [He even
          mouths the last part]

                    SKEETER
          Yes, ma'am.

                    BULA
          How much of the paper we got done?

                    SKEETER
          The front part's all done.

                                                    (CONTINUED)

CONTINUED: 51.

> BULA
> Then get it out there. The students are waiting.

> SKEETER
> [Mumbles to self] They all just love the school paper. [Exits]

> BULA
> Poor, Skeeter. This big time newspaper business is hard on the boy. [Looks through paperwork on desk] Now let's see. What do we have for next week's top story? Looks like we're down to two: Where is the school nurse sneaking off to during the day? Or who are the imaginary people the principal is always talking to? Wow. Where do we ever get such good news? I'll bet no other school paper can boast about these kind of headlines.

Monte the hall monitor rushes in with a fake gun.

> MONITOR
> (runs in, gun out)
> Hold it! Police!

> BULA
> Ah!

> MONITOR
> [laughs] Hey, Bula.

> BULA
> You scared me half to death.

> MONITOR
> I know. [snickers]

> BULA
> What you want, Monte?

> MONITOR
> You still paying a buck each for my hall monitor reports.

> BULA
> A buck a story. Offer's still good.

(CONTINUED)

CONTINUED:

> MONITOR
> [proud] I've got five this week.

> BULA
> Five! That's a regular crime wave.

> MONITOR
> You wouldn't believe what happens in these halls. If this keeps up, I may have to ask for an assistant.

> BULA
> Wouldn't that be something? [makes a note] That's a story in itself.

> MONITOR
> That's six bucks, then.

> BULA
> Fine. [Goes to purse] Six dollars. Don't you go spend that all in one place.

MONITOR exits.

> BULA
> [sarcastic] Boy, do I feel safe knowin' he's around. [Types] Crime wave hits the halls of our school. Hide your valuables. Monte the Hall Monitor says we had a record number of incidents this week. He caught one group of kids playing with firecrackers and trying to blow up the chemistry lab. He caught wrote over ten tickets for excessive farting in the gym. And rescued some guy from a locker that his girlfriend had stuffed in him. He must have done something pretty bad. Girl power gone wild. This school is out of control.

> KILABREW
> [enters] Bula? How's you feeling today?

> BULA
> Fine, fine. Here to bring me the school health report?

CONTINUED:

                    KILABREW
          Certainly. Oh, my.

                    BULA
          What?

                    KILABREW
          [examines BULA] You been getting
          enough vitamin C?

                    BULA:
          I... I don't know...

                    KILABREW
          YOU DON'T KNOW. Don't toy with your
          health, Bula. A healthy body is a
          temple for the gods.

                    BULA
          I thought there was only one God?

                    KILABREW
          You're so closed minded, Bula.

                    BULA
          What you got for me, Kilabrew?

                    KILABREW
          First, we have "This week's weight
          watch" by Nurse Nancy Kilabrew.

                    BULA
          You're not a nurse. You're just a
          student assistant.

                    KILABREW
          Whatever. See, I weigh all the
          athletes and I thought that would
          be something everyone would enjoy
          reading about. Emma Rogers - gained
          12 pounds. Patty May - lost 2
          pounds. And a big congrats to Jane
          Graham - Lost 25 pounds. And our
          football team's star lineman of the
          year, Billy Joe Bugle - happily
          gained another 27 pounds on his way
          to a school record 324 pound.

                    BULA
          Anything else?

(CONTINUED)

CONTINUED: 54.

> KILABREW
> Got some great baby names for you. I asked the art teacher, Mrs. Hicky, what she'd name her upcoming child. She has settled on naming the kid after her favorite snack: Goober if it's a boy.

> BULA
> And if it's a girl?

> KILABEW
> Raisinette.

> BULA
> Lovely.

> KILABREW
> That's six bucks.

> BULA
> Six? That's only two stories.

> KILABREW
> Four weight watchers and two baby names.

> BULA
> Five bucks then. The two names are for the same kid.

> KILABREW
> Fine. [BULA hands over $5] Oh, is that a bird I hear. Cheap, cheap, cheap.

> BULA
> You can go away now.

> KILABREW
> Cheap, cheap, cheap.

Kilabrew exits and Fanny appears at the door.

> FANNY
> Can I come in, Bula?

> BULA
> Why it ain't Fanny Mae Alcott? How is my favorite reporter today?

(CONTINUED)

CONTINUED:

>   FANNY
>   [Excited] Favorite reporter? Oooh.
>   That sounds good.
>
>   BULA
>   Well, you've been quite the news
>   hounds lately.
>
>   FANNY
>   News hound. I like the sound of
>   that too. The boys have always said
>   I've been a dog.
>
>   BULA
>   [Raises an eyebrow] Well...uh, what
>   you have for me today?
>
>   FANNY
>   Well, I was walkin' around looking
>   for a story. I went out behind the
>   boys locker room. I always go there
>   hoping to... uh... talk with one of
>   the boys. You know, interview 'em
>   after the big game. And if they
>   ever win a game, I'm gonna get the
>   best darn interview. Losing don't
>   make good news.
>
>   BULA
>   You got a point here, Fanny? I'm a
>   busy lady.
>
>   FANNY
>   I do. See I heard some of them boys
>   talking in the locker room. They
>   leave the window open cause it gets
>   real hot in there.
>
>   BULA
>   To the point, girl. A good reporter
>   gets to the point.
>
>   FANNY
>   [Hands over a report] Anyway, I got
>   this. Don't know if it's worth
>   printin.'
>
>   BULA
>   This is good.
>
>   FANNY
>   You think so?

(CONTINUED)

CONTINUED:

>BULA
>Top notch investigating.

>FANNY
>Gosh.

>BULA
>There's your dollar, darling. Enjoy.

>FANNY
>Wow. I feel just like Barbara Walters.

>BULA
>Keep it up and someday you just might be her.

>FANNY
>You really think so. I sure look up to her. Her and Jerry Springer.

>BULA
>They're the biggies.

>FANNY
>I'll see you tomorrow.

>BULA
>Keep 'em coming, Fanny Mae.

>FANNY
>I will. I'm headed over to the boys locker room. They got all kinds of interesting things going on over there.

>BULA
>This will do fine on the society page. [Sits at computer] Romance is a budding at the school. This week Jimmy Joe Johnson's heart is a palpitating for none other than Betty Sue Mall. Unfortunately he's feeling a bit shy and can't figure out a way to tell Betty he's got those special feelings for her. Don't you worry, though, Jimmy. She'll know all about it soon enough. Best wishes to both of you in this new found romance. Fanny Mae Alcott reporting.

(CONTINUED)

CONTINUED:

END OF SCENE

Principal enters.

> PRINCIPAL
> That looks more like creative writing than news. So that might be the end of our day at school but life goes on and the learning never ends. After school, our students scatter... teachers go to their second jobs... *(if audience reacts, principal can say: "because our school is labor of love and doesn't pay the bills. It'll be a good day when schools have all they need and doctors and lawyers have to do a bake sale to pay for their supplies.")* As the day grows old, some of our students gravitate to local hang outs such as coffee shops and book stores, while some utilize our local elegant restaurants for a first date.

SCENE 11: LOOKS GET IN THE WAY

There is a nice restaurant with a bit of a romantic atmosphere. A woman in a little old lady mask (Sidney) is sitting at the down center table sitting across from an empty chair. A man, Tony, walks up to the table. He stops and gives a funny look at Sidney.

> TONY
> Uh... I think I have the wrong table?

Sidney speaks in an old lady voice.

> SIDNEY
> Who you looking for, honey?

> TONY
> Sidney.

> SIDNEY
> That's me.

> TONY
> What?

(CONTINUED)

CONTINUED: 58.

                  SIDNEY
I'm Sidney.

                  TONY
Is this a joke?

                  SIDNEY
Are you Tony? You're late. I thought you'd be here at 12:15.

                  TONY
I've gotta go. Uh... I just wanted to tell you that Tony can't make it.

Tony leaves. Sidney does her regular voice.

                  SIDNEY
See you later, loser.

A waitress (or waiter) brings Sidney an appetizer. Sidney eats it through the mouth hole in the mask. Next Phil enters. He is a nerdy looking guy in glasses and has some old flowers in his hand. The waitress shows him to Sidney's table. Phil is so nervous he doesn't even look at Sidney and sits. He shields himself with his flowers.

                  PHIL
Hey, there, Sidney. I'm early. I mean I'm Phil and I'm early. I am glad you're early too, well, sort of. I was hoping to beat you and get used to things first. I get nervous in new situations. And with new people. I get nervous a lot. I brought you flowers.

Phil sticks the flowers in the middle of the table to it blocks Sidney from view and himself as well. Sidney tries to get a good look at Phil.

                  PHIL (CONT.)
The flowers are a little wilted. They were pretty. I mean there is this wonderful flower shop but I didn't have time to go there today but I did a few days ago and I wanted those flowers. I don't get a date every day you know and I wanted this to be special, so I got the best flowers I know of but I want this to be great. You know what I mean.

(CONTINUED)

CONTINUED: 59.

Sidney grabs and flowers and smells them. In her old lady voice she says:

                    SIDNEY
          They're lovely.

Phil sees Sidney's old lady mask for the first time. He is suddenly speechless. He stares a moment. He takes off his glasses and cleans them. He puts them on and looks again. Sidney puts the flowers to the side of the table and looks at Phil happily. After a few moments of silence:

                    PHIL
          What's with the mask?

                    SIDNEY
          Does it scare you?

                    PHIL
          Not really... it's just... weird.

                    SIDNEY
          Hmm... so you're not gonna run off
          on me?

                    PHIL
          I have to admit. I'm a little
          curious. Why would you wear an old
          person mask to lunch? And do the
          weird voice?

                    SIDNEY
          It's my way of weeding out the
          losers. I want to find a man who
          likes what I'm really like and
          doesn't let my looks get in the
          way.

                    PHIL
          Tell me about it.

                    SIDNEY
          You're not ugly.

                    PHIL
          I'm not?

                    SIDNEY
          Take off your glasses again.

Phil does and Sidney takes a very close look.

                                              (CONTINUED)

SIDNEY (CONT.)
You have very nice eyes.

PHIL
Really? You do too.

SIDNEY
Stop that.

PHIL
What?

SIDNEY
No physical stuff now.

PHIL
But you said my eyes... and your eyes are.. well... pretty...

SINDEY
No.

PHIL
But...

SIDNEY
Shoosh!

PHIL
Can't I?

SIDNEY
No.

PHIL
Okay.

Sidney looks very grumpy and crosses her arms. Phil looks around everywhere but at Sidney. After a few moments:

SIDNEY
The flowers are very nice.

PHIL
I like red. You like red?

SIDNEY
I'm not much in to colors.

PHIL
Why is that?

(CONTINUED)

CONTINUED:

> SIDNEY
> There's so loaded. Red is passion.
> Blue is sadness. Green is envy.

> PHIL
> It's good to feel something.

> SIDNEY
> Huh?

> PHIL
> A least those colors feel
> something. Black and white is so
> boring. No feeling at all.

Sidney nods approvingly and then holds out her appetizer.

> SIDNEY
> Hungry?

Phil takes something from the appetizer tray and eats it.

> PHIL
> Is that battered green beans?

> SIDNEY
> Uh-huh.

> PHIL
> That is my absolute favorite!

> SIDNEY
> No way.

> PHIL
> Nobody else likes these.

> SIDNEY
> I do.

> PHIL
> These are so good in the honey
> poppy seed sauce.

Sidney holds out some sauce.

> PHIL (CONT.)
> Oh, no you didn't?

Phil happily dips in the sauce.

(CONTINUED)

                    PHIL (CONT.)
          What are the odds we'd like the
          same things?

Sidney wiggles happily.

                    PHIL (CONT.)
          So... uh... what else happens on
          these dates? I mean... you seem to
          have had it all planned out with
          the mask and such. It's like a test
          or something. There was this one
          episode of Star Trek...

                    SIDNEY
          I like Star Trek...

                    PHIL
          Really?

                    SIDNEY
          Live long and prosper.

Waitress comes by.

                    PHIL
          Earl Grey tea... hot.

Waitress rolls her eyes and exits. Sidney is laughing.

                    PHIL (CONT.)
          So is this one of those Trekkie
          tests of the true nature of a
          species? What is the next trial?

                    SIDNEY
          Lunch?

                    PHIL
          Hmmm... I shall take this
          challenge.

Phil gets out a menu. He notices Sidney isn't looking.

                    PHIL (CONT.)
          Already know what you want?

                    SIDNEY
          Uh-huh.

                    PHIL
          What are you having?

(CONTINUED)

CONTINUED:

>   SIDNEY
>   It's a secret.

Phil puts down his menu and studies her.

>   PHIL
>   I'll take this challenge.

>   SIDNEY
>   What?

>   PHIL
>   I will take your lunch challenge.

Waitress appears.

>   SIDNEY
>   I'll have my usual.

Waitress turns to Phil.

>   PHIL
>   I too will have the unusual usual.

Waitress rolls her eyes and exits.

>   SIDNEY
>   You don't even know what it is.

>   PHIL
>   I am brave. I'll try anything once.

>   SIDNEY
>   It's very unusual.

>   PHIL
>   I didn't see anything too unusual
>   on the menu.

>   SIDNEY
>   My usual isn't on the menu.

Phil gets nervous.

>   PHIL
>   Oh.

Sidney laughs.

>   SIDNEY
>   Don't worry. It hasn't killed
>   anyone... yet. It is however
>   responsible for my lovely
>   appearance.

(CONTINUED)

CONTINUED:

Phil wrinkles his face.

              PHIL
I really don't want to look like that.

Sidney makes a hurt sound.

              SIDNEY
Oh... you bad man. You hurt my feelings.

              PHIL
Uh... uh... I'm sorry. I didn't mean to...

              SIDNEY
I was joking. Relax.

              PHIL
Maybe I should wear a mask on dates too. I get so nervous.

              SIDNEY
You're doing well.

              PHIL
It's the mask. It's helping me too for some reason. It's so ridiculous... I guess it lightens the mood.

Sidney makes another hurt sound.

              SIDNEY
Ri-dic, ri-dic... ri-dicles? Oh... my... I'm ridickles.

              PHIL
No, you've very normal. The rest of us are weird.

              SIDNEY
Darn tootin.

Waitress returns with a hot dog for each of them and then exits.

              PHIL
A hot dog?

(CONTINUED)

CONTINUED: 65.

>   SIDNEY
>   A hot dog.
>
>   PHIL
>   That is unusual for a nice
>   restaurant like this.
>
>   SIDNEY
>   And it is unusual. Who knows what's
>   in the meat.
>
>   PHIL
>   I actually love hot dogs.
>
>   SIDNEY
>   Really?
>
>   PHIL
>   Yup.

Phil devours it. Sidney watches in approval. After a few moments.

>   SIDNEY
>   Wanna see me without my mask?

Phil pauses. He looks nervous.

>   PHIL
>   Uh... I don't know... maybe... I
>   guess... this is a test too isn't
>   it. Oh man.

Sidney laughs and switches to her real voice.

>   SIDNEY
>   Don't be nervous. I'm not this
>   scary looking for real.
>
>   PHIL
>   Okay.
>
>   SIDNEY
>   I'm kind of ugly but nothing like
>   this.
>
>   PHIL
>   Ugly?
>
>   SIDNEY
>   Don't worry. I don't have a huge
>   nose or weird teeth or a huge mole
>   on my face. I'm just not very good
>   looking.

(CONTINUED)

CONTINUED: 66.

>   PHIL
>   I don't mind. I'm no William
>   Shatner.
>
>   SIDNEY
>   You sure?
>
>   PHIL
>   I'm sure I'm not William Shatner.

Sidney laughs and Phil joins her.

>   SIDNEY
>   You sure about the mask?
>
>   PHIL
>   I'm sure. I already know you have
>   beautiful eyes.
>
>   SIDNEY
>   Stop that.
>
>   PHIL
>   I still can't compliment you?
>
>   SIDNEY
>   No.

Sidney sits quietly a moment.

>   PHIL
>   You don't have to take off the
>   mask. It's okay.
>
>   SIDNEY
>   I want to. You're really nice. You
>   deserve to see my real face. You've
>   passed the test.

Phil waits nervously as Sidney removes the mask. Sidney looks shy and Phil look happy.

>   PHIL
>   You're beautiful.

Sidney does her old lady voice.

>   SIDNEY
>   No.
>
>   PHIL
>   You are... really.

(CONTINUED)

CONTINUED: 67.

                    SIDNEY
          Stop.

                    PHIL
          You don't have any reason to hide.

Sidney makes eye contact and returns his smile. They smile at each other happily a moment.

                    SIDNEY
          What another hot dog?

                    PHIL
          Sure.

                    END OF SCENE

Principal enters.

                    PRINCIPAL
          Things aren't always what they seem
          and it helps to not judge a book by
          it's cover. I hope you've enjoyed
          your visit here to our school, it's
          like no other... friendship,
          love... we've seen it all. We're
          here to help and pick you up when
          you fall. School is journey that
          you won't have to travel
          alone. And perhaps there something
          here that we've shown that will
          help you in the future too. And
          give you a bit of help in something
          you chose to do.

OPTIONAL EXTENDED ENDING

                    PRINCIPAL (CONT.)
          One more story? I think we have
          time. At times students need more
          help than the average joe... both
          students and the adults can use a
          little boost... and sometimes they
          help each other through some of the
          toughest times in life.

SCENE 12: MUCH MADNESS

Counselor's office... It's dark. The only light is from a door that opens offstage and we see Janey sitting in a chair. Two shadows from the doorway loom over JANEY. The first figure, DR. REID, speaks:

(CONTINUED)

CONTINUED:

                    REID
          She looks like she's barely alive.

                    NURSE
          She was refusing to eat anything. I
          finally got her to eat some bread
          and drink a little water though.

                    REID
          Thank you. I'll let you know how
          things go.
              (Crosses to Janey - REID's
               shadow grows as she enters the
               stage)
          Hello, Janey. I'm Dr. Reid your
          school counselor. (No
          response) What we need are some
          lights so we can see.

                    JANEY
              (Meekly)
          Please, no lights -

                    REID
          Okay.
              (Pause)
          How are you feeling? (JANEY glares)
          I see you're not too good today.
          (JANEY looks away) Do you feel like
          doing any talking? (JANEY shakes
          her head no) I hear you're not
          eating well. Can you tell me why?

                    JANEY
              (Pause)
          Bread and water suit me - I want
          nothing else.

                    REID
          I can get you something...

                    JANEY
              (Angrily)
          I don't want anything - and I don't
          want to talk anymore... I just want
          to be left alone.

Janey goes to window.

                    REID
          It's a beautiful day today.
              (Goes to JANEY)
          Would you like to go outside?
          (JANEY shakes her head no) Could I
              (MORE)

(CONTINUED)

CONTINUED:

              REID (cont'd)
at least open the window and let fresh air in? The rooms get stuffy on warm days. (JANEY nods. REID goes to window - opens it) There, it feels better already.

              JANEY
This is fine -

              REID
We have a group you can meet with. Would you like to join us?

              JANEY
No - I don't want to -

              REID
You might enjoy meeting some new people.

              JANEY
I said no -

              REID
I'm sorry, Janey. I'm just being friendly. I didn't mean to pressure you.

              JANEY
I know -

              REID
Would you like to go out and watch one of the teams practice?

              JANEY
      (Pause)
I want to be alone - I don't like being around lots of people - I get upset when there are crowds -
      (Pause. Looks at REID, afraid)
I get really scared - I almost feel like I can't breathe -

              REID
It is just a practice. There shouldn't be too many people there.

              JANEY
I just need to be alone, Dr. Reid -

(CONTINUED)

CONTINUED:

> **REID**
> You can't be alone forever. With me you'll be fine.
>
> **JANEY**
> (Angry)
> I can't be fine with anyone - you don't really care - you're simply doing your job - once I'm "better" you'll be through with me - then it's on to another student - you're just like anyone else -
>
> **REID**
> That's not true.
>
> **JANEY**
> (Almost shouting)
> I know it is - you probably haven't cared about any students in years - that would be unprofessional - and a burden you don't need for yourself -
>
> **REID**
> That isn't something I would do.
>
> **JANEY**
> Please, just let me go - I know what I need better than you -
>
> **REID**
> I don't know about that.
>
> **JANEY**
> You're not God, you know - you don't have the powers to cure everything - I know what you can and can't do -
>
> **REID**
> Janey, please calm down. Let's remember where we are at.
>
> **JANEY**
> Go on - get out now!
>
> **REID**
> Please, you need to relax.
>
> **JANEY**
> How can I will you in here bothering me all the time?

(CONTINUED)

CONTINUED:

Janey starts messing with a potted plant outside the window.

          REID
What are you doing?

          JANEY
Killing weeds -

          REID
Killing?

          JANEY
Cultivate beauty by killing the ugly - it's an odd practice - I do it now to know I won't do it again - in reality its weeds on which the soil feeds -
    (Stops)
But few people find the truth as fulfilling -

          REID
Do you like weeds?

          JANEY
Sometimes - If only you had planted something more useful - beans, or tomatoes, then the sacrifice might be worthwhile - but flowers, they're more difficult to justify -

          REID
Don't you think they satisfy any needs?

          JANEY
Frail beauty - that's all they are - cultivated for weakness - and has very little nutritional value - in the end they never can satisfy -

          REID
Many would disagree. I believe their beauty is food for the soul.

          JANEY
Frail and weak - a light frost would snap its neck -

JANEY breaks the head off a flower

CONTINUED:

> **REID**
> Janey, please...

> **JANEY**
> And so easily smitten by one little insect -
> *(JANEY holds up broken bud to a weed)*
> They choice is so easy - yet it's not -

> **REID**
> What do you mean?

> **JANEY**
> I suppose most people don't give it much thought -
> *(Looks up at sky)*
> I know a story of a man who had a plant which most called a useless weed - it turned out the weed was a cure for cancer - but the weed was nearly extinct so no one got the cure - do you believe in such a thing?

> **REID**
> I don't know. I suppose it's possible.

> **JANEY**
> But do you believe?
> *(Pause)*
> Oh, never mind - I guess to you most beliefs are only fables -

Throws both plants down - upset

> **JANEY (CONT.)**
> No one really cares, do they -

> **REID**
> Of course we do...

> **JANEY**
> They pay you to care - everywhere it's the same way -

> **REID**
> I wouldn't have taken this job if I didn't want to help people. And I wouldn't be here if I didn't want to help you.

(CONTINUED)

JANEY
Do you think you can help me?

REID
Only if you want me to.
(Pause)
Do you want my help, Janey?

JANEY
People should only fix what's broken -

REID
(Pause)
Why did you lock yourself in your house? If someone hadn't found you, you might have died.

JANEY
(Pause)
I had to -

REID
Why?

JANEY
I - I needed to - I had no choice - I had to get away - I couldn't live like others anymore -

REID
Why not?

JANEY
(Angry)
What do you want to know all this for?

REID
I'm sorry, Janey. We haven't talked enough...
(Pause)
But I think it's time we did.
(Pause) Did you lock yourself in the house because of your parents dying?

JANEY
(Furious)
I said I don't want to talk anymore! Leave me alone! I don't have to tell you anything! I'm not a little kid.

(CONTINUED)

(Bends over and buries her face in her hands

>   REID
>   (Concerned)
>   Are you crying?

>   JANEY
>   (Face still hidden)
>   No -

>   REID
>   You can't keep this inside you. You
>   need to get it out in the open.

>   JANEY
>   There's so much you don't know -

>   REID
>   Please, Janey, talk to me. You'll
>   be glad you did in the end.

>   JANEY
>   I just need to be alone - if only I
>   could fly -
>   (She looks up at the sky)

>   REID
>   I think the Earth is the best place
>   for you to do things you need to.

>   JANEY
>   No, I'm leaving all the Earthly
>   matters to you - I belong near a
>   different sun -
>   (Points to a star)
>   I wish I were a star - part of some
>   constellation so I would never be
>   lonely.

>   REID
>   Space would seem awfully lonely to
>   me. I don't think it would be much
>   fun.

>   JANEY
>   But it's so free - no one can touch
>   you or hurt you - you can simply
>   shine -

>   REID
>   You can shine here too.

(CONTINUED)

CONTINUED:

>   JANEY
>   People don't like it when you shine
>   - that's why stars are up there and
>   not down here - humans think
>   brightness is offensive -
>   (Pause - looks and smiles at
>   the stars)
>   My mother is a star now -
>
>   REID
>   Maybe.
>
>   JANEY
>   She always seemed like one to me -
>   but stars don't like it very well
>   where they can't be stars anymore -
>   (Pause - grows sad)
>
>   REID
>   Is something wrong, Janey?
>
>   JANEY
>   I want to be a star - stars having
>   meaning - stars I understand -
>
>   REID
>   I image we all would like to be
>   stars sometimes, but we know we
>   can't. Our only life is on this
>   Earth. There's no where else we can
>   go.
>
>   JANEY
>   Do you believe in an afterlife?
>
>   REID
>   (Pause)
>   Yes, I think so.
>
>   JANEY
>   Like heaven and angels and pearly
>   gates - free of all Earthly strife
>   -
>
>   REID
>   Maybe.
>
>   JANEY
>   I think it's a lot less defined
>   than that - I think maybe we all
>   end up a part of greater whole - a
>   tiny molecule in a bigger being or
>   a little star in a vast universe -
>   (MORE)

(CONTINUED)

JANEY (cont'd)
we'll return to where we came from - whether it's God, the Great Spirit, or something else - but I know that's where we will be -

REID
Faith can be very comforting.

JANEY
Everything around me seems to point to the same conclusion - "ashes to ashes - dust to dust" - where we begin is where we end - the Earth gives us life through what we eat and we give her life when we die - the source is the finish - rain that feeds the river comes from the sea - to each beginning there is a definable end -

REID
I'm speechless. You've been holding back.

JANEY
There's usually no one to listen - at least no one who's willing to bend -

REID
Does someone have to change their ways to listen?

JANEY
What's the use of talking if it doesn't do anyone any good?

REID
When you talk to someone, some change doesn't always have to happen.

JANEY
But I would do something if I could -

REID
It doesn't always work that way.

CONTINUED:

>   JANEY
>   Then why did you become a
>   counselor?
>
>   REID
>   (Long pause)
>   I haven't thought about why in a
>   long time. (Looks at JANEY) When I
>   started I knew how difficult it
>   would be. (Slight pause) But I
>   wanted to help people. I wanted
>   things to be better for people.
>
>   JANEY
>   That's good, Dr. Reid. It's good to
>   remember why.
>   (They look at each other in
>   silence - the lights fade to
>   black)
>
>   END OF SCENE

Principal enters

>   PRINCIPAL
>   Connections... that's what we
>   always hope to make in our
>   school. Connections to learning
>   and connections to each other. A
>   flower is beautiful but it wouldn't
>   exist without dirt. The dirt is
>   the soil that helps it grow and
>   develop. Sometimes we have to get
>   dirty and allow ourselves to seed
>   in the darkness in order to become
>   the beautiful blossom in the sun.

Another option scene.

>   PRINCIPAL (CONT.)
>   While many students are asleep,
>   getting rested for the next day,
>   some roam, looking for meaning...
>   lost in the darkness... rocked by
>   the sea of their unhappiness...
>   hoping to find a lifeline that will
>   pull them from the storm.

SCENE 13: FLOWERS IN THE DESERT

(Lights come up on the front of an old farm house. It is very early morning but the moon is full and the scene is well lit. As the scene opens, JIMMY comes stumbling on drunk. He drags on a ladder that he puts against the house JIMMY climbs the ladder. For staging purposes, the ladder can be put against stage R and the door to the house can simply be coming in from off stage])

                JIMMY
Where's my sweet little chicky?
She's gone and I'm all alone. Like
Rodeo and Juliet, split up by their
ma and pa, left with aching hearts.
I got an achky-breaky heart baby
and I'm coming for you.
    (Knocks on window)
I can hear you now. "Oh, Rodeo. Oh,
Rodeo. Where fartest you, Rodeo."
(Laughs at his own joke) Oh,
Juliet. (Knocks) Juliet! If you
don't come out, you gonna see
yonder window break.

                JAMIE
    (Appears at door below ladder.
    She is sleepy and cranky)
What do you want?

                JIMMY
Can Shelly come out and play?
    (Comes down ladder)

                JAMIE
She's asleep like I was before you
started banging on the window.

                JIMMY
    (Tugs on JAMIE's nightgown)
Can't you wake her up?

                JAMIE
No!
    (Smacks him)

                JIMMY
OW!

                SHELLY
    (Sleepy at door)
Who's out there, Jamie?

(CONTINUED)

CONTINUED:

                JAMIE
A sick loon. (Goes inside)

                SHELLY
       (Comes out)
Jimmy?

                JIMMY
Oh, hi, Shelly. Gosh, you look perdy.

                SHELLY
What are you doing out there? You're gonna get me in trouble.

                JIMMY
I need you, Shelly. I'm feeling lonely.

                SHELLY
You've been drinking. You know I don't like you when you're drunk.

                JIMMY
Oh, come on, Shelly. I've got needs you know.

                SHELLY
So do I and I need sleep. Now go away.

                JIMMY
I ain't leaving.

                SHELLY
Well, I ain't coming.

                JIMMY
I feel my heart about to break.
       (He starts a sick howl)
Owoooo!

                SHELLY
       (Covers his mouth)
Stop that! You'll wake Sarge.

                JIMMY
       (Pulls her to him)
I got you.

                SHELLY
       (Pushes him)
Quit playing around.

(CONTINUED)

CONTINUED:

> JIMMY
> (Starts to fall over)
> Look out below. (SHELLY grabs him) You do care. (He throws his arms around her)

> SHELLY
> (Pulls away)
> Stop it.

> JIMMY
> Why are you being so mean?

> SHELLY
> Me?

> JIMMY
> I just want a little love.

> SHELLY
> What you need is a cold shower and some coffee.

> JIMMY
> You're what I need, Shelly. Don't you need me?

> SHELLY
> What I need is a big club.

> JIMMY
> But Shelly. I'm hurting inside. Don't you care?

> SHELLY
> Not when you're like this.

> JIMMY
> (Angry)
> Fine. I'll go. Give me my ring.

> SHELLY
> What?

> JIMMY
> Give me my ring.

> SHELLY
> You don't mean it.

> JIMMY
> If you don't want me around, then I don't want you. Give it!

(CONTINUED)

CONTINUED:

>   (SHELLY sadly takes off ring)
>
>   SHELLY
>   (Gets a mischievous look)
>   Fetch boy.

She throws it off R.

>   JIMMY
>   Oh, man.
>   (Runs off R)
>
>   JAMIE
>   (Pokes her head out)
>   Is he gone?
>
>   SHELLY
>   (Sad)
>   Uh-huh.
>
>   JAMIE
>   Are you okay?
>
>   SHELLY
>   (Sits and rubs her finger)
>   No. (Holds out hand) I gave him
>   back his ring.
>
>   JAMIE
>   You did?
>   (Crawls out)
>
>   SHELLY
>   Maybe I should have gone with him.
>
>   JAMIE
>   But he was so drunk. He smelled
>   like a sick skunk.
>
>   SHELLY
>   Oh, he always smells like that.
>   (They laugh a little)
>   I really love him, Jamie, but
>   sometimes... sometimes he can be
>   such a creep.
>
>   JAMIE
>   There's a lot better guys in the
>   world. Once you get out of here,
>   you'll see that.

(CONTINUED)

CONTINUED:

>   SHELLY
> But that's just it, Jamie. All the
> guys I've met are creeps. I attract
> them like flies to manure.
>
>   JAMIE
> Don't say that. You're a lot better
> than manure.
>
>   SHELLY
> Thanks, I think.
>
>   JAMIE
> That didn't come out right.
>   (Sound inside)
> What was that?
>
>   SHELLY
> Get down.
>   (They hide as SARGE comes out)
>
>   SARGE
> Is somebody out here?
>   (Sees girls)
> What are you girls doing?

SHELLY turns with a smile to face SARGE.

>   SHELLY
> We got up early to see the sunset.
>
>   JAMIE
> Sunrise.
>
>   SHELLY
> Sunrise. I've been bragging to
> Jamie so much about it she just had
> to see it.
>
>   SARGE
> And how would you know how nice
> they are? You're never up this
> early.
>
>   SARGE
> Do I see a ladder? How did that get
> there?
>
>   SHELLY
> A ladder? Gee, I don't know. Did
> you know there was a ladder there,
> Jamie?

(CONTINUED)

82.

CONTINUED: 83.

                    JAMIE
Come on, Shelly. I'm tired. Let's go back to bed.

                    SARGE
Sounds like a good idea to me.
         (JAMIE goes inside. But SHELLY
         won't budge)

                    SARGE
Shelly?

                    SHELLY
What is this, a prison camp? Can't a girl have a few moments to herself?

                    SARGE
Inside... now.

                    SHELLY
But Sarge...

                    SARGE
Back inside now or I might find out the real reason you're up so early.
         (SHELLY looks worried and
         heads inside)

                    JIMMY
         (JIMMY enters R with a bag on
         his head)
Now, Shelly. You said you didn't want to see me anymore. With this bag on my head I can't see you so does that count? (Goes up and hugs SARGE) Come on. You can forgive me, can't you? (Pause) Did you put on a little weight or something? (Backs up and feels SARGE's arms) You've been working out too. (SARGE pulls the bag off JIMMY's head) Oh, no.

                    SARGE
         (Pointing at steps on porch)
Sit.

JIMMY does. SARGE stares at JIMMY a minute

                    JIMMY
Are you gonna kill me, Sarge?

                                              (CONTINUED)

CONTINUED:

                    SARGE
          I'm thinking about it.
               (Pause. JIMMY is very nervous)
          What were you doing up there? And
          don't lie to me. I was once a
          pretty good liar myself, so I know
          one when I see one.

                    JIMMY
          I guess I had a little too much to
          drink.

                    SARGE
          Right under your parent's noses...

                    JIMMY
          Man, they don't care. You should
          see them sometime. Talk about
          drunk.

                    SARGE
          But you're just a kid.

                    JIMMY
          I'm almost 18. And I only have two
          years of high school left.

                    SARGE
          You may not make it to 18 if you
          keep this up.
               (JIMMY gets quiet)
          What were you doing over here?

                    JIMMY
          I was looking for Shelly.

                    SARGE
          I thought so.

                    JIMMY
          Then why'd you ask?

                    SARGE
          Don't get mouthy.

                    JIMMY
          Sorry. It's the booze talking.

                    SARGE
          Well, it better stop talking or
          it's going to get dunked into the
          water trough.

                                              (CONTINUED)

CONTINUED:

>   JIMMY
>   We didn't do nothing, Sarge. Shelly
>   didn't want to.
>
>   SARGE
>   She didn't?
>
>   JIMMY
>   She didn't want to get in trouble.
>   Man, was she mean to me.
>
>   SARGE
>   She was?
>
>   JIMMY
>   (Mad)
>   All we did was fight. I made her
>   give my ring back.
>
>   SARGE
>   The promise ring?
>
>   JIMMY
>   Yeah. But she threw it somewhere.
>   Now I can't find it.
>
>   SARGE
>   (Walks out and gets ring)
>   It's right over here.

Hands it to JIMMY

>   JIMMY
>   Maybe it's a sign. Maybe Shelly and
>   me is supposed to make up.
>
>   SARGE
>   Maybe so. Maybe not.
>   (Pause)
>   I'm not sure I want you around
>   Shelly anymore.
>
>   JIMMY
>   Oh.
>
>   SARGE
>   But she really likes you and if she
>   wanted to be with you she'd find a
>   way.
>   (Paces)
>   The more I'd tell Shelly she can't
>   see you, the more she'd find times
>   to sneak away. (Studies JIMMY) So
>   (MORE)

(CONTINUED)

                    SARGE (cont'd)
          maybe we can take care of this some
          other way.

                    JIMMY
                (Nervous)
          Uh... like how?

                    SARGE
          Growing up, I did a lot of stupid
          things too. My mother died when I
          was real young and my pappy didn't
          want to take care of me. So my
          family sent me around, hoping
          somebody could handle me, but I
          only got worse. My big moment was
          in a barn. I burnt it down. That's
          when my Aunt Minnie took me in. And
          for the first time somebody loved
          me no matter what I did wrong. Even
          though I didn't change over night,
          that love stuck with me. And as I
          grew older, that love became more
          and more a part of me until all the
          hate was gone.

                    JIMMY
          So what's your point?

                    SARGE
          The point is, Jimmy, that you need
          some love. Not the kind of love
          you're thinking about, but a caring
          kind of love.

                    JIMMY
          Don't get all sappy on me, Sarge.

                    SARGE
          I want to help you, Jimmy. I want
          to help you be a better person.

                    JIMMY
          I want to be good. I always want
          to, but it's hard. Was it hard for
          you?

                    SARGE
          It took more than 30 years to learn
          to be a good person.

                                        (CONTINUED)

CONTINUED:

                    JIMMY
          Thirty years?

                    SARGE
          More probably. I stopped counting.
               (Frowns at the memories)
          I used to have some awful habits.
          Drinking, smoking, gambling.
          Gambling was the worst. I gave up
          the other things with no problem,
          but gambling... I still can't even
          look at a deck of cards.

                    JIMMY
          How did you finally give it up?

                    SARGE
          I don't know that I have. A few
          years ago I was caught up in it
          again. Some old friend invited me
          over and they thought what I'd love
          was a game of poker cause that's
          what we used to do together. Of
          course they talked me into playing.
          What a terrible night.

                    JIMMY
          You lost big, huh?

                    SARGE
          No, I won.

                    JIMMY
          How much?

                    SARGE
          Several hundred dollars.

                    JIMMY
          Really? Cool.

                    SARGE
          No, it wasn't. I felt the old
          desires coming back. I was secretly
          planning to sneak away to a casino.
          I never did spend any of the money
          though. I couldn't.

                    JIMMY
          Do you still have it?

(CONTINUED)

CONTINUED:

> **SARGE**
> No. I felt too guilty. I did the only thing I could think of to make up for it.
>
> **JIMMY**
> What?
>
> **SARGE**
> I gave it to our church.
>
> **JIMMY**
> All of it?
>
> **SARGE**
> All of it.
>
> **JIMMY**
> Too bad.
>
> **SARGE**
> So are you willing to give something up for Shelly?
>
> **JIMMY**
> Like what?
>
> **SARGE**
> Drinking maybe.
>
> **JIMMY**
> But all my friends drink.
>
> **SARGE**
> Maybe you need different friends.
>
> **JIMMY**
> Everyone will think I'm a total loser.
>
> **SARGE**
> Shelly won't.
>
> **JIMMY**
> (Sighs. Looks at ring)
> I guess I could give it a try.
>
> **SARGE**
> No. Either you will or you won't. There's no "in the middle."

(CONTINUED)

CONTINUED:

> JIMMY
> (Thinks)
> Okay. I will. For Shelly.

> SARGE
> Go home and sober up. Then we'll talk some more.

> JIMMY
> Okay, Sarge. And thanks...

> SARGE
> For what?

> JIMMY
> For not killing me.

JIMMY exits and SARGE chuckles.

Principal enters.

> PRINCIPAL
> As everyone heads off to bed, we say good-night. The moon rises in the sky... such a beautiful sight. We pray for tomorrow to be a better day. We dream of finding the perfect path to the true way. The way to a better future for us all. A future where we can be proud and stand tall.
>
> So will you go gently in to that good night? Or will you rage against the dying of the light?

> EXCELSIOR

Made in the USA
Columbia, SC
07 August 2020